ESCAPE FROM EXTINCTION

ANDREW KITCHENER & KATE CHARLESWORTH

HMSO EDINBURGH & NATIONAL MUSEUMS OF SCOTLAND

"BECAUSE OF **HUMAN ACTIVITIES**, THE **RATE** OF **EXTINCTION** OF PLANT & ANIMAL SPECIES IS **SPEEDING UP**. THE ENVIRONMENT CAN COPE WITH **SOME** EXTINCTIONS, BUT TOO **MANY**, TOO **FAST**, COULD **TOTALLY WEAKEN** THE EARTH'S **LIFE-SUPPORT** SYSTEMS".

FROM THE PERMANENT EXHIBITION, 'WORLD IN OUR HANDS' AT THE **ROYAL MUSEUM** OF **SCOTLAND**, CHAMBERS STREET, EDINBURGH.

AKNOWLEDGEMENTS TO:

JOHN BURTON, JOHN HARTLEY, DAVID UNWIN.
VANESSA NIAS, CLARY CHARLESWORTH.

PUBLISHED BY HMSO: EDINBURGH
& THE NATIONAL MUSEUMS OF SCOTLAND, EDINBURGH.

© TRUSTEES OF THE NATIONAL MUSEUMS OF SCOTLAND 1993
FIRST PUBLISHED 1993
PRINTED IN SCOTLAND FOR HMSO & THE NATIONAL MUSEUMS OF SCOTLAND
ISBN 0 11 495122 5

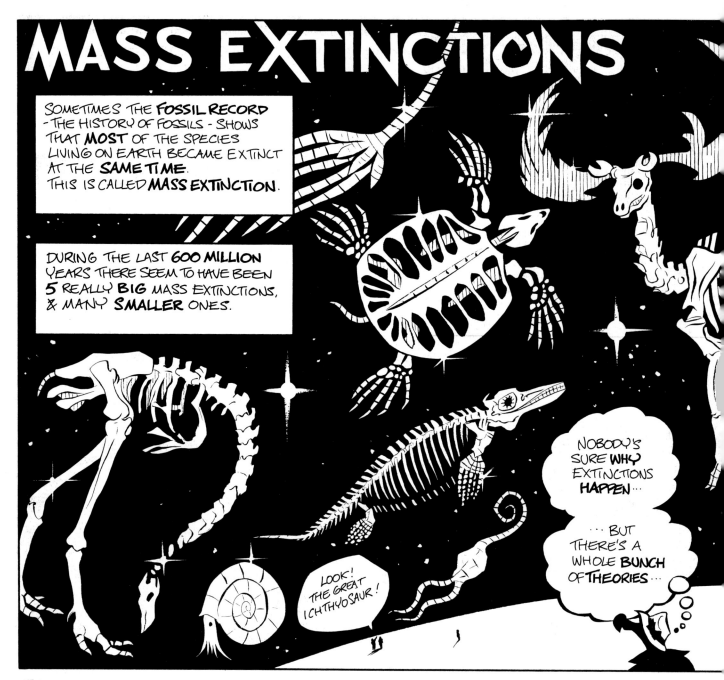

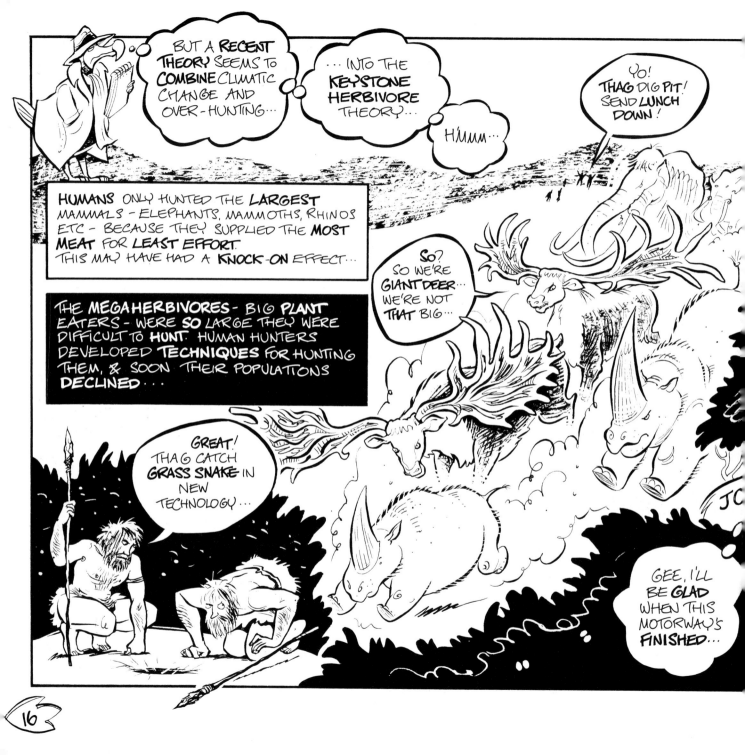

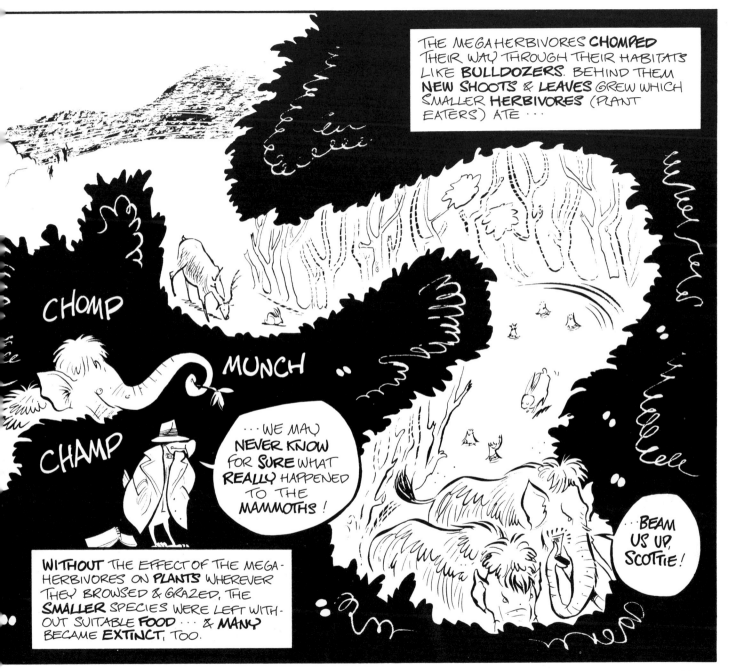

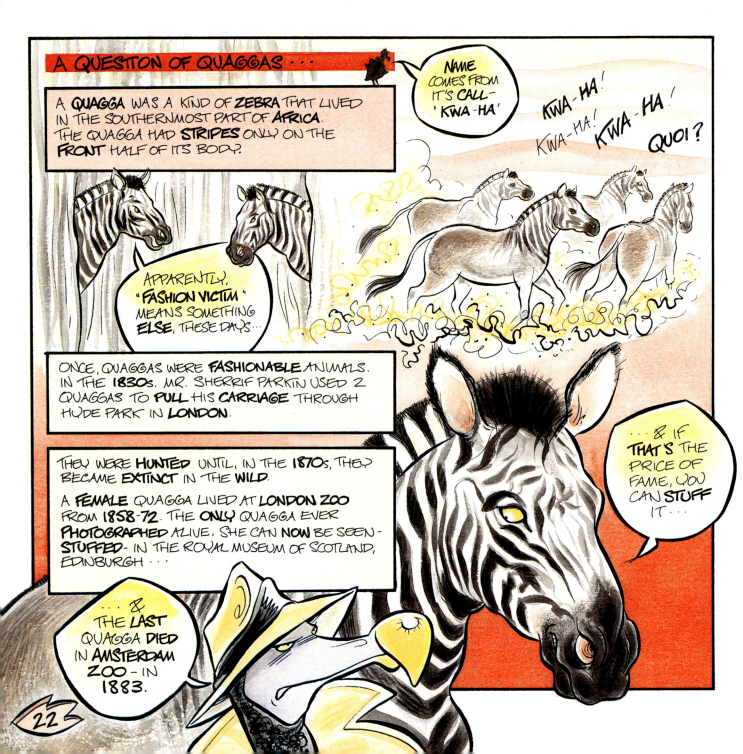

WHERE'S THE WOLF?

THE **TASMANIAN WOLF**, OR **THYLACINE**, WAS A MARSUPIAL MAMMAL. IT WAS PROBABLY **ALREADY** EXTINCT IN AUSTRALIA BY THE TIME EUROPEANS SETTLED THERE, BUT IT **STILL** LIVED IN **TASMANIA**.

IT WAS SOON THE VICTIM OF **SHEEP** FARMERS BECAUSE IT **KILLED** THEIR SHEEP. IN **1888** THE GOVERNMENT OFFERED A **REWARD** FOR EACH ANIMAL KILLED.

BY **1914**, THE DEATH TOLL WAS **2268**.

BY 1936, THE THYLACINE WAS GIVEN LEGAL PROTECTION — **TOO LATE**. THE **LAST KNOWN** ANIMAL DIED IN HOBART ZOO **2 MONTHS** LATER.

SOME PEOPLE **STILL** REPORT SEEING THE THYLACINE IN AUSTRALIA & TASMANIA, BUT **MOST** SCIENTISTS BELIEVE IT IS **EXTINCT**.

ALL OVER THE WORLD, ANIMALS & PLANTS ARE **STILL** EXPLOITED FOR **FOODS, OIL, TIMBER, FUR** & MANY OTHER PRODUCTS.

MANY **MILLIONS** OF WILD ANIMALS ARE SOLD EVERY YEAR AS **GOODS** & **PETS**...

THIS TRADE IS STILL A GREAT THREAT TO THEIR **SURVIVAL**...

LOOK! IT'S THE LAST ONE! — BASH IT'S HEAD IN!!

DIDN'T A DOG GET GRANDMA?

IT'S HARDLY SURPRISING. THEY DID IT TO THE PEOPLE WHO FIRST LIVED HERE, TOO...

MIXING BLOOD

EXTINCTION SOMETIMES HAPPENS WHEN THE **LAST INDIVIDUALS** OF A SPECIES **INTERBREED** WITH A **CLOSELY-RELATED** SPECIES. THE **AUROCHS** (WILD CATTLE) PROBABLY BECAME EXTINCT BY **HYBRIDIZING** - MIXING - WITH **DOMESTIC CATTLE**.

THE **NEW ZEALAND BLACK STILT** IS NOT EXTINCT **YET**... ONLY ABOUT **50** BIRDS SURVIVE. BUT THE **LAST** ONES ARE BREEDING WITH THE CLOSELY-RELATED **PIED STILT** - WHICH **COULD** RESULT IN ITS EXTINCTION.

PLAGUE, PESTILENCE & POISON...

THE **ACCIDENTAL** INTRODUCTION OF **DISEASES**, **PESTICIDES** - WHICH KILL INSECTS & PESTS - & **OTHER** POISONS TO AN ENVIRONMENT CAN CAUSE EXTINCTIONS.
MANY OF THE LAST **CALIFORNIA CONDORS** WERE KILLED BY **POISON** PUT OUT FOR "**PESTS**". IN 1985, THE **LAST 27** BIRDS WERE **CAUGHT** & TAKEN INTO **CAPTIVITY** FOR **BREEDING**.

SEVERAL SPECIES OF **HAWAIIAN HONEY-CREEPERS** HAVE DIED OUT AFTER CATCHING **BIRD DISEASES**, SUCH AS **AVIAN MALARIA**, FROM IMPORTED **PIGEONS**...

NEW TECHNIQUES ARE BEING USED:
ARTIFICIAL INSEMINATION –
THIS IS A WAY OF GATHERING SPERM FROM A MALE ANIMAL. THE SPERM IS THEN PLACED INTO THE FEMALE TO FERTILIZE HER EGGS.
A GIANT PANDA IN LONDON ZOO NEVER MET THE MOTHER OF HIS BABY BORN IN MADRID...

EMBRYO TRANSFER –
AN EGG CAN BE TAKEN FROM THE MOTHER, FERTILIZED, & GIVEN TO A REPLACEMENT MOTHER. AT CINCINNATI ZOO A FRIESIAN COW GAVE BIRTH TO A GAUR CALF IN THIS WAY...

BUT CAPTIVE BREEDING IS DIFFICULT & EXPENSIVE, & DOESN'T SOLVE ALL THE PROBLEMS.

HABITATS MAY DISAPPEAR – THERE'S NOWHERE SAFE FOR THE GUAM RAIL OR HAWAIIAN GOOSE TO LIVE.

THERE'S A DANGER OF IN-BREEDING WEAKENING THE OFFSPRING, WHICH MAY CAUSE A SPECIES TO BECOME EXTINCT IN CAPTIVITY.

& SOME ANIMALS MAY HAVE TO BE TAUGHT HOW TO LIVE IN THE WILD...
EG THE GOLDEN LION TAMARIN...

WHAT D'YOU MEAN, 'CONGRATULATIONS'?

WELL! WHO'D HAVE THOUGHT YOU'D HAD IT IN YOU?!

WILL THE WILD BE LIKE EURODISNEY, MUM? WILL IT? WILL IT?!?

H'MM... SOME PEOPLE THINK IT'S POSSIBLE TO BRING BACK EXTINCT SPECIES... LIKE MAMMOTHS...

HUH!

DAILY MUCK
T-REX CLONE ATE MY HAMSTER!

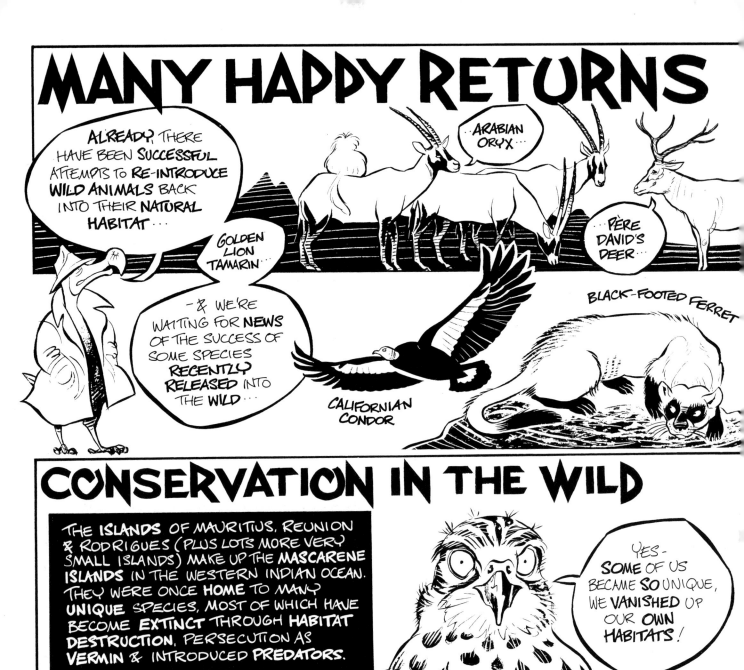

PROTECTED AREAS...

CAPTIVE BREEDING & RE-INTRODUCTION CAN ONLY SAVE A FEW OF THE MOST ENDANGERED SPECIES. MOST CAN ONLY SURVIVE IF THEIR NATURAL HABITATS ARE PROTECTED OR LOOKED AFTER FOR THEIR BENEFIT.

THE WORLD'S FIRST NATIONAL PARK WAS STARTED IN 1872 AT YELLOWSTONE, USA. IT PROTECTS A SPECTACULAR LANDSCAPE OF MOUNTAINS, HOT SPRINGS & GEYSERS, AS WELL AS ITS WILDLIFE, INCLUDING THE GRIZZLY BEAR...

NOW THERE ARE 5000 PROTECTED AREAS IN THE WORLD - THAT'S GOOD, BUT THAT'S ONLY 4% OF THE LAND AREA ON EARTH & SOME OF IT IS ALREADY BEING TAKEN OVER BY PEOPLE HUNGRY FOR FOOD & WOOD. WE STILL NEED TO DO MUCH MORE:

MOST PROTECTED AREAS ARE TOO SMALL, ESPECIALLY FOR LARGE ANIMALS. MORE THAN 93% ARE LESS THAN 5000 KM² - BUT A PACK OF WOLVES MAY NEED 12,000 KM² TO ROAM OVER...

& THESE AREAS CAN PROVIDE NO GUARANTEE THAT EVEN PROTECTED ANIMALS, ALIVE & WELL, ARE NOT WIPED OUT BY SOME NATURAL OR HUMAN-MADE DISASTER.

"THIS PLACE IS JUST GREAT... WE COULD GET A FANTASTIC PRICE, GUYS - WHY DON'T WE SELL UP & MOVE OUT TO VEGAS?!"

NATIONAL PARKS
HOT SPRING
JAKUZZI
bears onlie

IN 1982 THE WORLD CONGRESS OF NATIONAL PARKS DECIDED TO SET UP A WORLD SYSTEM OF PROTECTED AREAS COVERING 10% OF THE EARTH BY 1992. IN 1993, HALF OF THIS TARGET HADN'T BEEN ACHIEVED.

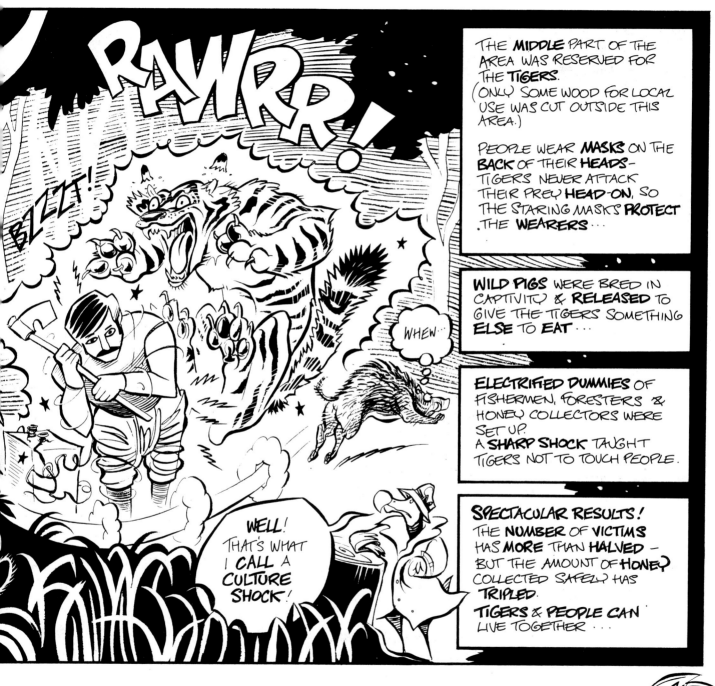

The **PROGRAMME** FOR BELIZE...
...WAS SET UP IN **1989** TO DO JUST THAT IN THIS TINY **CENTRAL AMERICAN** COUNTRY.

A **HUGE** AREA OF RAINFOREST IN THE NORTH OF BELIZE IS NOW **PROTECTED**.
IT EARNS **MONEY** FOR THE COUNTRY BY ENCOURAGING **TOURISTS**.

THERE ARE ALSO PLANS FOR **EXPERIMENTS** IN SUSTAINABLE **CUTTING** OF TREES & EXTRACTION OF **PRODUCTS** IN WAYS THAT DO NOT **HARM** THE FOREST.

"WELL... THEY'VE GOT TO BE ROUND HERE SOMEWHERE..."

GLOBAL ANSWERS TO GLOBAL QUESTIONS

"...AND I'VE BEEN IN 'LIFE ON EARTH'..."

"MANY PARROTS ILLEGALLY TRADED! MANY PARROTS ILLEGALLY..."

TRADE: HOW CAN IT BE STOPPED?
AN INTERNATIONAL AGREEMENT WAS SET UP IN **1973** - **CONVENTION** ON **INTERNATIONAL TRADE** IN **ENDANGERED SPECIES** OF WILD FAUNA & FLORA - **CITES**.
CITES AIMS TO **CONTROL** OR EVEN **BAN** TRADE IN THE WORLD'S ENDANGERED ANIMALS & PLANTS. BUT TO **SUCCEED**, ALL COUNTRIES MUST **WORK TOGETHER**.
THERE IS STILL A **HUGE** ILLEGAL TRADE IN ANIMALS & PLANTS, BUT CONTROLS **HAVE** HELPED.

THE **NORTHERN ELEPHANT SEAL** - DOWN TO **50** AT THE **BEGINNING** OF THE 20TH CENTURY NUMBERED **50000** IN THE **1990**S BECAUSE **HUNTING** WAS **BANNED**...

GARDEN HABITAT

If you have a **GARDEN**, flowers, bushes & trees give **FOOD** & **SHELTER** to animals. You could even make a small **POND** for frogs & newts & water insects.

But a **WINDOWSILL** of flowers will also attract animals like butterflies, moths, bees & birds.

LITTER

...Daisy had **CROAKED** ...seen off by a deadly **POT-NOODLE**...

Litter can **HARM ANIMALS**, or worse, **KILL** them. Don't leave it **LYING AROUND**.

COLLECTING

Never be tempted to **TAKE HOME** living things — take **PHOTOGRAPHS** instead!

DON'T BUY anything made of **IVORY**, **CORAL**, **REPTILE** skins or **TORTOISE-SHELL**... they are all from **LIVING CREATURES** ...& anyway — it's **ILLEGAL**!

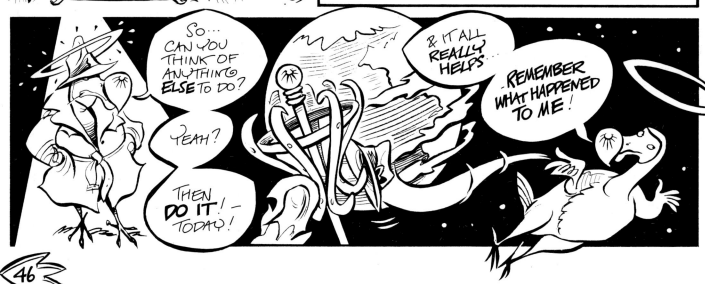

So... can you think of anything **ELSE** to do?

Yeah?

Then **DO IT!** — Today!

& it all **REALLY HELPS**...

...remember what happened to me!

Q? INDEX

ACCIDENTS:	DO THEY HAPPEN?	4
AGRICULTURE:	WHY CAN IT BE A PROBLEM?	29
AUROCHS:	WHAT WERE THEY?	28
A BANG:	— OR A WHIMPER?	12
BELIZE:	WHY IS IT IMPORTANT?	43, 44
BIRDS:	WHICH WERE THE HEAVIEST EVER?	19
CALIFORNIAN CONDOR:	WHY ARE WE WAITING FOR NEWS?	28, 36
CAPTIVE BREEDING:	HOW CAN IT HELP?	33
CITES:	WHAT DOES THIS STAND FOR?	43
CLIMATE:	CAN IT CHANGE?	9, 14
COMPETITION:	WHAT DO ANIMALS COMPETE FOR?	7
DANGER LIST:	WHAT IS ON IT?	30
DESERT ISLANDS:	WHY ARE THEY RISKY?	26
DINOSAURS:	DID THEY COMMIT SUICIDE?	11
DINOSAURS:	HOW LONG DID THEY TAKE TO DISAPPEAR?	13
DODOS:	WHEN DID THEY BECOME EXTINCT?	27
DOMESTIC ANIMALS:	HOW CAN THEY CAUSE DESTRUCTION?	20
DWARF MAMMALS:	WHY WERE THEY UNIQUE?	18
EARTH:	WHAT HAPPENED WHEN IT MOVED?	13
ECOTOURISM:	HOW DOES IT WORK?	44
EVOLUTION:	DOES IT EVER STOP?	6
EXPLOITATION:	WHAT ARE SOME OF THE PRODUCTS WE GET FROM … ANIMALS & PLANTS?	24
EXTINCTION:	IS IT FOREVER?	3, 35
EXTINCTION:	IS IT NATURAL?	6, 7
EXTRA-TERRESTRIALS:	COULD THEY HAVE CAUSED EXTINCTIONS?	9
FOSSIL RECORD:	WHAT CAN IT TELL US?	8
GASTRIC BROODING FROG:	WHEN WAS IT LAST SEEN?	30
GENES:	CAN THEY SURVIVE EXTINCTION?	35
GIANT MAMMALS:	WHO WERE THE GIANTS?	14, 18
GIANT SABLE ANTELOPE:	WHERE IS IT THE VICTIM OF WAR?	31
GREAT AUK:	WHAT WIPED IT OUT?	21
HABITATS:	WHAT DESTROYS THEM?	29, 31
HABITATS:	WHAT SAVES THEM?	38, 39
HAWAII:	WHAT HAS GONE FOR EVER IN HAWAII?	19
HOMELESS:	WHAT MAKES ANIMALS HOMELESS?	29
HUNTING:	WHEN DID HUMANS GET GOOD AT IT?	15
HYBRIDIZING:	WHAT'S GOING ON?	28
ICE-AGES:	HOW MANY WERE THERE?	14
ICE-AGE GIANTS:	WHAT WERE THEY?	16
INTRODUCTIONS:	WHO WAS INTRODUCED TO WHAT?	25
IVORY:	SHOULD YOU BUY IT?	46
JAVAN RHINO:	HOW MANY ARE THERE LEFT?	30

LEGAL PROTECTION:	WHAT WAS IT TOO LATE FOR? 24
LITTER:	IS IT A KILLER? 46
MAMMOTHS:	WHO ATE THEM? 15
MARSUPIALS:	WHAT HAVE THEY GOT THAT WE HAVEN'T? 25
MASS EXTINCTIONS:	HOW MANY HAVE THERE BEEN? 8
MAURITIUS:	WHAT'S GOING ON? 36, 37
MEGAHERBIVORE:	WHAT IS IT BESIDES BIG? 16
MIXING BLOOD:	HOW DOES IT HAPPEN? 28
MOAS:	HOW TALL WERE THEY? 19
MODERN EXTINCTIONS:	WHEN DID THEY START? 20
MUSEUMS:	WHAT ANIMALS ARE ONLY IN MUSEUMS? 5
MYOTRAGUS:	WHY DID IT HAVE SHORT LEGS? 18
NATIONAL PARKS:	ARE THEY BIG ENOUGH? 39
PAPER:	HOW CAN YOU SAVE IT? 45
PASSENGER PIGEON:	WHO WAS MARTHA? 3, 23
POISON:	WHAT WAS KILLED BY POISON? 28
POLLUTION:	WHAT SUBSTANCES ARE DANGEROUS? 31
PREDATORS:	A MEANS OF SURVIVAL? 7
PREVENTION:	WHY IS IT BETTER THAN CURE? 42
PROTECTED AREAS:	ARE THERE ENOUGH? 39
PTEROSAURS:	DID THEY FLY? 10
QUAGGA:	WHY IS IT SPECIAL? 35
RAINFORESTS:	HOW MANY SPECIES LIVE IN THEM? 32
RAINFORESTS:	HOW FAST ARE THEY DISAPPEARING? 32
RECYCLING:	WHAT'S IT ALL ABOUT? 45
RE-INTRODUCTION:	HOW SUCCESSFUL IS IT? 36, 39
ROUND ISLAND REPTILES:	WHAT SAVED THEIR HABITATS? 38
SAFARIS:	HOW DO THEY HELP? 44
SAFE SPACE:	WHO NEEDS IT? 40
SEA COWS:	HOW EASY WERE THEY TO CATCH? 21
SEA DRAGONS:	ARE THEY STILL ALIVE? 12
SNUB:	WHY SHOULD YOU DO IT? 45
SPECIES:	WHAT IS A SPECIES? 4
SUCCESS STORIES:	WHAT HAS BEEN WILDLY SUCCESSFUL? 36, 37, 38
SUN BLOCK:	WHAT CAUSED IT IN 1870? 23
TASMANIAN WOLF:	DEAD OR ALIVE? 24
THEORIES:	HOW HAS EXTINCTION BEEN EXPLAINED? 9, 10, 11, 12, 13
TIGERS:	WHY DID THEY GO TO SCHOOL? 40
TIMBER:	CAN WE HAVE TIMBER & RAINFORESTS TOO? 42
WATER:	WHAT SHOULDN'T GO DOWN THE DRAIN? 45
WHALES:	WHY IS WATCHING THEM GOOD? 44
WILDLIFE TRADE:	HOW CAN IT BE STOPPED? 43
WOLVES:	HOW MUCH SPACE DOES A PACK OF WOLVES NEED? 39
WRENS:	WHO ATE THE WRENS FROM STEPHEN ISLAND? 26
YELLOWSTONE PARK:	WHAT'S SPECIAL ABOUT THE LANDSCAPE? 39
YOU:	WHAT CAN YOU DO? 45
ZOOS:	WHAT PART DO THEY PLAY? 33

DID T-REX BITE?